Go through with God, thy vows to pay,
thy life upon the altar lay;
the Holy Ghost will do the rest,
and bring to thee God's very best!

Known by Jesus

A quest for intimacy with Jesus Christ

AUTHOR

Andrew McIlroy

Saints & Scholars Publishing

ISBN-13: 9781093285277

Dedication

To Mum and Dad who introduced me to Jesus.
Thank you.

CONTENTS

Prologue – The Cry of my Heart

I have a longing in my heart that is becoming almost all-consuming. I cry with the Psalmist, *"O God. Display your power, O God as you have in the past."* (Psalm 68:28) I desire to see the sinner saved from sin, to see the captive set free from prisons of addiction, sickness and all the devices and demonic powers of the devil.

God has created within me an intolerance of the indifferent, mediocre, powerless Christianity that is prevalent all around us.

God has created within me an intolerance of the flaky and false that so often passes for Spirit-filled Christianity.

God has created within me a hunger for the real and authentic that Jesus demonstrated when He met the deepest needs of those He encountered with Living Water and the Bread of Life as He went around doing good and healing all who were oppressed by the devil (Acts 10:38.)

God has created within me a desire for the real and authentic that Jesus promised that we, today, could see and experience when He declared *"anyone who believes in me will do the same works I have done, and even greater works, because I am going to be with the Father"* (John 14:12.)

I cry with Paul *"I want to know Christ and*

experience the mighty power that raised him from the dead" (Philippians 3:10) I want to see the supernatural power of God, signs, wonders and miracles in Jesus' name. I want to be able to say with Peter *"this Good News has been announced to you by those who preached in the power of the Holy Spirit sent from heaven"* (1 Peter 1:12) and with Paul *"my message and my preaching were very plain. Rather than using clever and persuasive speeches, I relied only on the power of the Holy Spirit"* (1 Corinthians 2:4) leading to the result that *"they were convinced by the power of miraculous signs and wonders and by the power of God's Spirit. In this way, I have fully presented the Good News of Christ"* (Romans 15:19)

Perhaps this is the longing of your heart also, and I pray that it is, then listen carefully to this warning. I was walking, praying, and contemplating these things when God spoke His word deep into my heart. Hear the word and warning of God. Jesus says that *"on judgment day many will say to me, 'Lord! Lord! We prophesied in your name and cast out demons in your name and performed many miracles in your name.'"* That is my desire, to prophesy in Jesus' name, to cast out demons in Jesus' name to perform many miracles in Jesus' name. But then Jesus went on to speak to these specific people these terrifying, awesome words,

"But I will reply, 'I never knew you. Get away from me, you who break God's laws.'" (Matthew 7:21-23)
Listen to those alarming words, spoken to people who claimed to have seen the very things that I long to see,

"I NEVER KNEW YOU!"

This is what God spoke into my heart and this is what I want you to hear and understand, that above all, Jesus wants to know us. He desires an intimate personal relationship with us. Then out of that place of intimacy will flow the supernatural power of God.

As I pondered these things, the cry of my heart became,

"I WANT TO BE KNOWN BY JESUS."

And from that cry, these words and thoughts flowed that has become this little book.

Introduction:

Imagine being in the crowd on that hillside out there beside the Sea of Galilee. You have been listening to the wonderful teaching of Jesus for so long that you forgot about food, but now you are getting hungry. You watch carefully as something is happening. The disciples have brought a small lunch to Jesus, He takes it and seems to be praying. He breaks it and gives it back to the disciples. Now they are bringing it to the people sitting in rows. How could so little feed so many? And yet it does not seem to be running out. A disciple comes closer to you, and you reach out to receive. You eat until you're full, and still there is more. On your way home you think to yourself, *"I met Jesus, I heard Him teach, and I ate miracle food that He took and blessed, it doesn't get any better than this,"* or does it?

In Acts chapter 1 when the disciples are discussing who should replace Judas, Peter makes it clear that it needs to be someone who was *"with us the entire time we were travelling with the Lord Jesus — from the time he was baptized by John until the day He was taken from us. Whoever is chosen will join us as a witness of Jesus' resurrection."* What an unspeakable privilege to have walked that journey with Jesus.

This group would seem to have been the seventy that we read about in the Gospels. Right from His baptism, through all the teachings and miracles, the ugliness of the cross, the wonder of the resurrection, to the joy of meeting the risen Jesus. Would that be enough, would that satisfy the deep longing of your heart to have had that awesome experience?

But what about the twelve? Especially chosen and called by Jesus. Hand-picked as it were. For three years, Jesus poured His life into this group. These were the men who would carry on His mission after He returned to Heaven. These are the men that are still known, spoken about and that we call our children after to this very day. Can you imagine what it would have been like to have been one of the twelve?

From within this group of twelve, there emerged a smaller group of three. It appears that Jesus was especially close to this little group. They seem to have been more intimate with Jesus than any of the others. On four special occasions, Jesus included them in unique experiences. They were there when He raised Jairus' daughter back to life (Luke 8:51). They witnessed His power over death and His compassion, gentleness and care for the little girl. They stood with Him on the mount of transfiguration (Matthew 17:1) where they received a glimpse of the full glory and majesty of Jesus. *"We have seen his glory, the glory of the Father's one and only Son,"* recollected John (John 1:14). *"We saw his majestic splendour with our own eyes,"* said Peter (2 Peter 1:16.) Along with Andrew, they had a private conversation with Jesus on the Mount of Olives (Mark 13:3) when He shared with them the inner secrets of God. And it was this three, Peter, James and John that He invited to go further with Him into the Garden of Gethsemane allowing them to witness His suffering and to glimpse something of the cost of salvation.

Out of that three one stands out. John describes himself as the *"disciple that Jesus loved."* John 13:5 pictures John leaning on Jesus, resting his head on Jesus as he asks Him a question. John had that cherished place of intimacy with our Lord. Perhaps the most moving scene is when Jesus was dying on the cross: *"When Jesus saw his mother standing there beside the disciple he loved, he said to her, "Dear woman, here is your son."* And he said to this disciple, *"Here is your mother."* And from then on this disciple took her into his home."*(John 19:25-27) Jesus entrusts His beloved mother's future to John, who chose the place of intimacy with Jesus. Certainly, this speaks of a special place Jesus held in John's heart. On resurrection morning, Mary Magdalene discovered the empty tomb and ran to tell Peter and John and the other disciples. The one Jesus loved, John outran Peter to the tomb and was the first disciple to see it empty. John was also the first to recognize Jesus after Jesus' resurrection. Some of the disciples were fishing and didn't realize it was Jesus on the shore. *"Then the disciple Jesus loved said to Peter, "It's the Lord!"* (John 21:7.) It would seem since John spent so much time in the Lord's presence, that he was able to recognize the Lord when the other disciples— including Peter and James in the inner circle—did not? It seems it was love that drew John into deeper intimacy with Jesus. This is the same John who wrote 1 John declaring God is love….

"See what great love the Father has lavished on us…" (I John 3:1a).

"This is how we know what love is: Jesus Christ laid down his life for us…" (I John 3:16a)

"We love because he first loved us" (I John 4:19).

Multitudes, Seventy, twelve, three, one!

In which group would we be found?? Each of the disciples was as close to Jesus as he chose to be, for Jesus had no favourites. Their relationship with Him was the result of their own choice, conscious or unconscious. There was nothing about James and John with their desire for prominence and position that commended them to Jesus. There was nothing about Peter with his volatile temperament and ultimate denial that earned him a place in the inner circle.

How did John gain that place of pre-eminence in the group? Was it because he alone took the place of privilege that was available to all? It was love that drew John into deeper intimacy with Jesus than the other apostles. Jesus loved them all, but John alone adopted the title "*the disciple Jesus loved*."

"The place on Jesus' breast is still vacant and open to any who are willing to pay the price of deepening intimacy. We are now, and we will be in the future, only as intimate with God as we really choose to be."
J. Oswald Sanders

<u>One</u>

Starting Afresh – Leave behind what you have learned.

"Who is the King of glory? The LORD of Heaven's Armies--He is the King of glory." **Psalm 24:10**

Sometimes we have to unlearn in order to learn. Man was created in the image of God and the danger is that we repay the favour and seek to make God in our image. We can have in our mind a Jesus that has been shaped by myth, misconception and our life journey. A Jesus of convenience; a Jesus that suits what we want Him to be. Perhaps a white middle-class Jesus that thinks just the way that we do!

How does my Jesus, your Jesus compare with the Jesus that John the Baptist was beheaded for, that Peter was imprisoned for, that Paul died for? Have you ever stopped to think about why the fundamental terrorist has such allegiance to their false cause that they will blow themselves up with a suicide bomb, but the faith that most Christians have means that they struggle to meet together with other believers once a week never mind actually tell anyone about Him?

It was a beautiful autumn day. I was in England for a family wedding and spending a day visiting the historic university city of Oxford. My time was limited, and I had a list of things that I wanted to see in the short time available. High on the list was the original painting of Holman Hunt, Jesus Light of the World (Painted in 1853). This is the image of Jesus standing outside a closed door gently knocking seeking admittance. Entering the Chapel at Keble College, I made my way into a small room where my guide book said it was located. And there it was, hanging on the end wall. The room was dark, and the painting was roped off so that you couldn't get close to it. Here I was standing in front of this world-famous painting of Jesus that I had seen in reproduction since I was a child and being honest, I was underwhelmed and more than slightly disappointed.

Is that the way, perhaps you feel about Jesus? You think that He should be so much more, but as yet you haven't seen that reality. I turned to leave that room in Keeble chapel when a small sign on the side wall caught my eye. It simply said, "**To illuminate the painting press the switch.**" So I did as it said and pressed the switch turning to face the painting. For a second, nothing changed. Then slowly LED lighting began to illuminate the painting until there it was in all of its glory. It was a breath-taking and emotionally moving moment. What I had struggled to see was now made clear in all of its glory.

Can I ask you, "**Is Jesus just a shadowy figure in the gloom to you?**" My prayer is that through these pages the Holy Spirit will bring you into the full light of the Lord Jesus Christ.

Sometimes we need to unlearn in order to learn. And the longer we have learned something the harder it is to unlearn. For many, we have learned half-truths or untruths about Jesus. They are ingrained into our minds and are keeping us in the dark to the extraordinary reality of the glory of Jesus.

On outreach one afternoon as I spoke to a lady, she looked at me and said, "*I believe in the man on the cross.*" Now that at face value sounds good. But I discerned that what she was putting her faith in was a crucifix image hanging on a wall. I gently said, "*do you know dear, Jesus isn't on the cross anymore.*" She looked at me in puzzlement and replied, "*Where is He then?*" Her Jesus was a dead man on a cross. How many have a Sunday School Jesus? A gentle Jesus meek and mild. This Jesus is far from the wild Messiah that is portrayed in the pages of the Bible. For many others, Jesus is just a baby in a manger with donkeys and shepherds looking on and a somewhat strange link with Santa Claus.

The illustrations on the pages of Children's Bibles and storybooks can also have a lasting impact on our view of Jesus. Many in the western world have been greatly influenced by Walter Sallman's (1940) image of a very white western Jesus with long flowing blonde hair. I remember the 2001 BBC special about what Jesus may have looked like. In this program, forensic scientists took a skull from first-century Palestine and, using the reconstructive techniques of police investigators constructed the face of a typical Jewish man in Palestine 2000 years ago. Just an ordinary swarthy-skinned man. One of the things that I have often pondered is that after three years of public ministry the religious leaders in Jerusalem needed Judas to betray Jesus with a kiss. As the prophet Isaiah taught, "*there was nothing beautiful or majestic about his appearance, nothing to attract us to him.*" Jesus had no special physical features and obviously wore no distinctive clothing that marked Him out as different. This image of an ordinary Middle Eastern man may not be popular with the white western church but it is symbolic of the many myths that we need to unlearn to get to the truth of the real Jesus.

The problem is, how do we know if what we are believing is the truth or not? I remember reading of how a bank trained their cashiers to recognize counterfeit money. You might think that they spent a long time examining different types of false notes but on the contrary, all they do hour after hour, day after day, is handle authentic currency until they are so familiar with the true that they cannot possibly be fooled with the false. I was teaching a camp of teenagers on the topic of the Christian Soldier. One morning we looked together at the lesson on the Sword of the Spirit. To illustrate its use, we considered some of the lies that the devil tells teenagers and then we cut those lies to pieces with the Sword of the Spirit, the truth of the Word of God. God began to move powerfully in that meeting by His Spirit and a profound work was done in the lives of many of those young people. We need to allow the Sword of the Spirit to cut out any and all wrong beliefs that we have about Jesus and to replace them with the mighty truth of the Word of God.

It is so clear to my heart that we must have a Jesus that is worth falling in love with. A Jesus that is worth surrendering our lives for. A Jesus that we willingly live every moment of every day for. We need to see Him as the King of glory. C.S. Lewis speaks of this in *The Lion, The Witch, and The Wardrobe* when Mr. Beaver tells Susan that Aslan (the ruler of Narnia) is a great lion. Susan is surprised since she assumed Aslan was a man. She then tells Mr. Beaver, *"I shall feel rather nervous about meeting a lion."* She asks Mr. Beaver if Aslan is safe, to which Mr. Beaver replies, *"Safe? Who said anything about safe? 'Course he isn't safe. But he's good. He's the King."* It is time to leave behind a safe Jesus made in our mind and experience and to fall in love afresh with the one who angels worship, ***"and there were loud voices shouting in heaven: "The world has now become the Kingdom of our Lord and of his Christ, and he will reign forever and ever."***

May our desire be like those men who came to Philip and the cry of their heart was *"**Sir, we would see Jesus.**"* That from the very depths of our innermost being we would cry:

"Open the eyes of my heart Lord, I want to see You, I want to see You;
To see You high and lifted up Shining in the light of Your glory.
Pour out Your power and love.
As we sing holy, holy, holy."

Oh that the Holy Spirit would draw aside the veil and allow us to see Him.

To see Him –

Compassionate - Kneeling with the woman taken in adultery, touching the leper, weeping over Jerusalem. *"A bruised reed He will not break, And smoking flax He will not quench, Till He sends forth justice to victory;"* (Matthew 12:20)

Courageous – *"As the time drew near for him to ascend to heaven, Jesus resolutely set out for Jerusalem."* Luke 9:51 *"looking unto Jesus, the author and finisher of our faith, who for the joy that was set before Him endured the cross, despising the shame, and has sat down at the right hand of the throne of God."* (Hebrews 12:2)

Challenging - Continually breaking religious traditions, killing sacred cows. He declared *"My kingdom is not of this world. If My kingdom were of this world, My servants would fight, so that I should not be* *delivered to the Jews; but now My kingdom is not from here."* (John 18:36)

Conquering – *"Let me now remind you, dear brothers and sisters, of the Good News I preached to you before. I passed on to you what was most important and what had also been passed on to me. Christ died for our sins, just as the Scriptures said. He was buried, and he was raised from the dead on the third day, just as the Scriptures said."* (1 Corinthians 15)

Up from the grave He arose,
With a mighty triumph o'er His foes
He arose a Victor from the dark domain,
And He lives forever with His saints to reign.
He arose! He arose!
Hallelujah! Christ arose!   (Robert Lowry)

Coming again - *"Men of Galilee,"* they said, *"why are you standing here staring into heaven? Jesus has been taken from you into heaven, but someday he will return from heaven in the same way you saw him go!"* (Acts 1:11)

The longer you have been a Christian the danger is that the more misconceptions that you have to unlearn. As I have been a Christian for over 30 years, I speak to myself as much as to any reader. I think God understood that this would be our problem. It was the story when He came to earth.

Even the disciples, after walking with Jesus for 3 years, entering all that they saw and heard failed to grasp the reality of the nature and mission of Jesus. They misunderstood the cross and were confused by the resurrection. It all didn't make sense to them, that is, until the day of Pentecost.

God knows our frame and all our weaknesses. It was for this very reason He sent His Holy Spirit to earth. *"When the Spirit of truth comes, he will guide you into all truth. He will not speak on his own but will tell you what he has heard. He will tell you about the future"*(John 16:13). I do not think that the Apostles fully understood all that Jesus did and taught and was until the Day of Pentecost. If that is true how can you and I ever hope to understand who Jesus is without that revealing, truth giving, guidance that only comes from the Holy Spirit?

We need to set aside everything we have learned if it does not stand completely on what the Bible the Word of God tells us. The Apostle Paul met Jesus in a very real and definite way on the road to Damascus. He was converted. His life was changed. He could have spent the rest of his life, doing what many today do, telling of how he had been such a bad man doing terrible things but then he met Jesus, and Jesus changed his life. What a tragedy it would have been if Paul had stopped with a conversion experience. Paul moved on from there to the desert for three years, during which time the Holy Spirit instructed him in the ways of God. He emerged, ready to communicate divine truth. Towards the end of his life, he was still pursuing deeper intimacy with Jesus as we hear his hearts cry

– That I may know Him.

Dear friend is it possible that you have grown complacent in your pursuit of Jesus? If we were sitting together over a cup of coffee and I was to look you in the eye and ask, *"Was there ever a time that you were more passionate, more in love with Jesus than you are now?"* What would your answer honestly be? Or it could be the reality that you have never know Jesus in this way, an intimate personal way. Jesus is calling you to start again, to leave behind what you have learned and to launch out into a new adventure of falling in love with Him, of growing in intimacy and knowledge of His love and care for you.

Sit in the quiet of your soul for a few minutes and listen, ponder, meditate on the voice of Jesus speaking directly to you:

Then Jesus said, *"Come to me, all of you who are weary and carry heavy burdens, and I will give you rest. Take my yoke upon you. Let me teach you, because I am humble and gentle at heart, and you will find rest for your souls. For my yoke is easy to bear, and the burden I give you is light."* (Matthew 11:28-30)

Then Jesus said to his disciples, "If any of you wants to be my follower, you must give up your own way, take up your cross, and follow me. If you try to hang on to your life, you will lose it. But if you give up your life for my sake, you will save it. And what do you benefit if you gain the whole world but lose your own soul? Is anything worth more than your soul? (Matthew 16:24-26)

"But I have this against you, that you have abandoned the love you had at first. Remember therefore from where you have fallen; repent, and do the works you did at first. He who has an ear, let him hear what the Spirit says..." (Revelation 2)

What kind of love is this that gave itself for me?
I am the guilty one, yet I go free.
What kind of love is this, a love I've never known;
I didn't even know his name – what kind of love is this?

What kind of man is this, that died in agony?
He who had done no wrong was crucified for me.
What kind of man is this, who laid aside his throne
that I may know the love of God – what kind of man is
this?

By grace I have been saved; it is the gift of God.
He destined me to be his own such is his love.
No eye has ever seen, no ear has ever heard,
nor has the human heart conceived what kind of love is
this?

(Words by Bryn and Sally Haworth)

Two

Saturated in the Word – Learning the truth.

"Jesus replied, "I am the bread of life. Whoever comes to me will never be hungry again. Whoever believes in me will never be thirsty." (John 6:35)

You are an extremely privileged and blessed person. I am presuming that if you have access to this book and the ability to read it or listen to it being read then you also have access to the book all about Jesus and the ability to read it or listen to it being read. As you ponder this great gift that has been given to you remember that with privilege comes responsibility. To whom much has been given much will be required.

This chapter is not a theological treatise or a character study on the life of Jesus. After all, I am urging you to set aside what you have been taught by man or what you have read that may not correctly line up with the Bible. My goal is to encourage you to go to the source and help you draw from the truth to bring you in to this place of intimacy with Jesus.

We live in a day of rapid communication. Email, Facebook and a multitude of mobile apps make the sharing of information around the world almost instantaneous. I am old enough however, to remember the pleasure that a handwritten letter from a family member or loved one brought. I particularly remember times at Bible College in Edinburgh, how that during our morning break that days post was distributed. If there was a letter for me, I can say with no fear of contradiction that letter was read. It wasn't thrown in the drawer or unto the shelf and forgotten about. It was read and thought about and re-read. Today someone may send you a message by mobile phone text. You then may be asked the question, *"Did you get my text?"* The implication is clear. The expectation is that if you received the text, you read the text. Isn't that true? Jesus Christ has sent us His text, the precious Word of God and yet I have to ask you this question-

Have you and are you reading it?

If we are to unlearn the wrong that we have taken on-board, we must learn the truth about Jesus. The place to learn this truth is not from some gifted teacher or insightful book as helpful as that might be. The place that we need to make as our priority, our first port of call, is the text that Jesus has given unto us, His Word.

Job declared – "*I... have treasured his words more than daily food.*" (Job 23:12) Until we begin to place this sort of priority on our meditation of the Bible we will not gain the results we desire. When last did we say to ourselves, "*Well, I had a big feed a few days ago, I don't need to eat today.*" Just as our consumption of food is regular and often so our meditation on the Bible ought to be consistent and often.

There is a similar picture in the book of Revelation. John tells us, "*Then the voice from heaven spoke to me again: "Go and take the open scroll from the hand of the angel who is standing on the sea and on the land." So I went to the angel and told him to give me the small scroll. "Yes, take it and eat it," he said. "It will be sweet as honey in your mouth, but it will turn sour in your stomach!" So I took the small scroll from the hand of the angel, and I ate it!"* (Revelation 10:9-10)

John walks up to the angel and asks for the book. The angel hands it to him, but gives him the clear instructions, *"eat it, eat the book."* And that is exactly what John does. John eats the book. He doesn't just scan or skim through it. He takes it right into himself, he assimilates it into his very being. If the Bible is to be more to you than just an interesting story about God, it must be internalized. The angel does not tell John that he should learn and pass on information about God. He tells him to take it right into his being so that when he speaks, the words are coming out from his very essence, his innermost being.

One Christmas several years back we took our children on a special visit to the Zoo. There were lots of seasonal festivities going on. The children had great fun wrapping up presents for the Chimpanzees then hiding them in their enclosure as they were safely shut outside. The Chimps were as excited as my kids on Christmas morning as they were let back into their enclosure. It was comical watching them find, open then eat or play with their gifts. Then we moved on to the Lion enclosure. With the lions securely locked up, the zookeeper placed several big parcels all nicely wrapped up in

Christmas paper around the pen. Then he released the male lion and two females. The big lion sniffed around several of the parcels before settling on the one he wanted. With one swipe of his enormous paw, he ripped the end of the wrapped box and stuck his head inside devouring whatever bone or meat he found there. As he was focused on his goodies, one of the lionesses walked towards him. Without moving his head out of the box the lion uttered a deep throaty growl and the lioness understanding the meaning turned and walked away. *"Stay away, this is mine, I am giving it my undivided attention."* The prophet Isaiah makes a similar observation in chapter 31 where he states, *"As a lion growls, a great lion over its prey –and though a whole band of shepherds is called together against it, it is not frightened by their shouts or disturbed by their clamour."*

What is really interesting is that the word the prophet uses to describe the lion's growl is the Hebrew word *'hagah.'* This word is usually translated as *'meditate'* in the Old Testament. In Psalm 1 as the Psalmist is describing the blessed man or woman, he says they are those that **"delight in the law of the Lord,"** on which *"he meditates day and night."* It is the same word that is used in Psalm 63, *"I lie awake thinking of you, meditating on you* *through the night."* What if we approached our Bible reading like this? Chewing it; devouring it; not letting anyone or anything distract us from it; not letting go until we have taken it into ourselves. Is this what the Psalmist has in mind when he states, *"Taste and see that the Lord is good."* (Psalm 34:8)

Some things to keep in mind –

The Bible is a Spiritual book. I was speaking recently to a minister who had completed a theological degree at a denominational college. He told me of how the Bible was treated as a textbook, just like other textbooks to be studied and not as the revealed Word of God. Jesus says to us in John 6:63 *"the very words I have spoken to you are spirit and life."* The words of the Bible are not just letters they are also spirit. Remember what Jesus said in John 4:24, *"For God is Spirit, so those who worship him must worship in spirit and in truth."* Jesus is teaching this key principle: God is Spirit, and man can only touch Him with his spirit. This principle is the same when we come to the Bible. Since God's Words are spirit, we have to read them in spirit. We can only really grasp spiritual things with the spirit. The Bible is not like an ordinary book just with words and letters printed on paper. The very nature of the Bible is spirit. Because of this we must approach it with our spirit and read it with our spirit. The spirit is needed to worship God and the spirit is needed to read the Bible in the way that it needs to be. Without the spirit, we cannot know God and without the spirit, we cannot know the Bible either. Until our Spirit is regenerated at Salvation by the Holy Spirit the Bible can be no more to us than an interesting history book.

Listen again to the words of Jesus, *"The Spirit alone gives eternal life. Human effort accomplishes nothing. And the very words I have spoken to you are spirit and life."* (John 6:63) In the realm of the spirit, everything is living and profitable, in the realm of the flesh or human effort, everything is unprofitable. We cannot study the Bible only with our mind and intelligence but it must be studied with our spirit also.

In order to help us understand this let's look at another passage of Scripture – 1 Corinthians 2. Look at verses 1 to 4: *"When I first came to you, dear brothers and sisters, I didn't use lofty words and impressive wisdom to tell you God's secret plan. For I decided that while I was with you I would forget everything except Jesus Christ, the one who was crucified. I came to you in weakness—timid and trembling. And my message and my preaching were very plain. Rather than using clever and persuasive speeches, I relied only on the power of the Holy Spirit."* The topic of this chapter is that Paul's preaching is not with persuasive words of wisdom. Listen to the next verses. *"I did this so you would trust not in human wisdom but in the power of God. Yet when I am among mature believers, I do speak with words of wisdom, but not the kind of wisdom that belongs to this world or to the rulers of this world, who are soon forgotten. No, the wisdom we speak of is the mystery of God—his plan that was previously hidden, even though he made it for our ultimate glory before the world began."* And also verses 9 to 13: *"That is what the Scriptures mean when they say, "No eye has seen, no ear has heard, and no mind has imagined what God has prepared for those who love him." But it was to us that God revealed these things by his Spirit. For his Spirit searches out everything and shows us God's deep secrets. No one can know a person's thoughts except that person's own spirit, and no one can know God's thoughts except God's own Spirit. And we have received God's Spirit (not the world's spirit) so we can know the wonderful things God has freely given us. When we tell you these things, we do not use words that come from human wisdom. Instead, we speak words given to us by the Spirit, using the Spirit's words to explain spiritual truths."*

Where was Paul's revelation coming from? His

revelation came from the Holy Spirit because only the Holy Spirit knows the things of God. How can we have this revelation from the Holy Spirit? Paul tells us that in order for us to have it we must have the Spirit of God. Paul is making it clear that spiritual things can only be communicated to spiritual people. He puts it quite bluntly in verse 14: *"But people who aren't spiritual can't receive these truths from God's Spirit. It all sounds foolish to them and they can't understand it, for only those who are spiritual can understand what the Spirit means."*

How to read the Bible spiritually?

We need to have a complete reliance on God to do for us what we cannot do for ourselves. We must have a supernatural divine intervention to enable us to internalize and be transformed by the Bible. To learn what we need to know about Jesus, simply put, we need Jesus to teach us.

On the Emmaus Road, two disciples were perplexed by all that had happened in the last days of Jesus's life. So Jesus spoke, *"And he said to them, "O foolish ones, and slow of heart to believe all that the prophets have spoken! Was it not necessary that the Christ should suffer these things and enter into his glory?" And beginning with Moses and all the Prophets, he interpreted to them in all the Scriptures the things concerning himself."* (Luke 24:25-26) Jesus attributed their lack of understanding of who He was to their foolishness and slowness of heart. When they arrived at their home, Jesus revealed Himself to them, then vanished. They said to each other, *"Did not our hearts burn within us while he talked to us on the road, while he opened to us the Scriptures?"* (v.32) Later he met with the eleven and said to them, *"Then he said to them, "These are my words that I spoke to you while I was still with you, that everything written about me in the Law of Moses and the Prophets and the Psalms must be fulfilled." Then he opened their minds to understand the Scriptures."* (vs.44-45)

Jesus helps these disciples by first opening the Scriptures and secondly opening their minds to understand them.

God shines supernatural light into our hearts. Paul writes: *"For God, who said, "Let there be light in the darkness," has made this light shine in our hearts so we could know the glory of God that is seen in the face of Jesus Christ"* (2 Corinthians 4:6). At the beginning of the world, God created light in the darkness, in a similar way God creates light in the human heart – the light of the knowledge of Jesus Christ that through Him we might know the glory of God.

God supernaturally enlightens our hearts to grasp what the Scriptures reveal. *"...that the God of our Lord Jesus Christ, the Father of glory, may give to you the spirit of wisdom and revelation in the knowledge of Him, the eyes of your understanding being enlightened; that you may know what is the hope of His calling, what are the riches of the glory of His inheritance in the saints, and what is the exceeding greatness of His power toward us who believe, according to the working of His mighty power which He worked in Christ when He raised Him from the dead..."* (Ephesians 1:17-18 NKJV) Without this supernatural help, we will not see in the Scriptures the glory and beauty of Jesus that is really there.

As we come to the Bible we need to ask and rely on Jesus to reveal Himself to us through the sacred pages, as we read, meditate, savour, taste, digest and take into our very being the knowledge of Him. Determine to be saturated in the Word – Learning the truth.

"The statutes of the Lord are right, rejoicing the heart;

The commandment of the Lord is pure, enlightening the eyes;"

(Psalm 19:8)

Three

Soaked in Worship – Loving Jesus.

"We love Him because He first loved us."
(1 John 4:19 NKJV)

Worship is the natural response of our very being to what we are learning about Jesus Christ.

Did you hear about the couple that got married accidentally? I googled it just to check but I don't think it has ever happened. What is my point? Intimacy doesn't just happen, it takes time, effort, planning and deliberate choices of the will. If we want to get to a place of intimacy with the Lord Jesus Christ then worship is an essential pathway.

The Pharisees met together and came up with a plan. They went to Jesus and one of them, an expert in religious law, tried to trap him with this question: He asked Jesus, *"Teacher, which is the most important commandment in the law of Moses?"* Jesus replied, *"'You must love the Lord your God with all your heart, all your soul, all your mind, and all your strength.' This is the first and greatest commandment."* (Matthew 22:37,38; Mark 12:30)

This is biblical worship. Loving Jesus with our mind. Focusing on Him, who He is, what He has done for us. With our heart, our emotions. With our soul. The soul refers to your personal spirit. This is the eternal part of your being. When the first human being was created, he was given a physical body, but he was not considered "alive" until a spirit was put inside of him, referred to as the breath of life, which caused him to become a living soul. Our strength, our very body is to be used to worship Him.

We were created to worship God, but when man turned away from God and sin entered the world, we began to worship anything but God. This is how the apostle Paul puts it: *"And instead of worshiping the glorious, ever-living God, they worshiped idols made to look like mere people and birds and animals and reptiles. So God abandoned them to do whatever shameful things their hearts desired. As a result, they did vile and degrading things with each other's bodies. They traded the truth about God for a lie. So they worshiped and served the things God created instead of the Creator himself, who is worthy of eternal praise! Amen."* (Romans 1) When we turn our affection away from God then we ascribing worth and worship to other things besides God.

It is so easy to allow this slide to take place. To allow our love for Jesus to cool off and to begin to place our affections in other areas. This is what had happened to the Church in Ephesus and earned them a rebuke from Jesus: *"But I have this complaint against you. You don't love me or each other as you did at first! Look how far you have fallen! Turn back to me and do the works you did at first."* (Revelation 2) The clear call that came to the Church at Ephesus and that comes to my heart and yours is -

REPENT

Jesus is calling us to turn back to Him. He doesn't want anything to break or hinder our relationship with Him.

John, the one who leaned on Jesus' breast at the Last Supper was very concerned about intimacy. He has a favourite word, *"abide,"* which means *"stay close to, remain in close fellowship with."* That is where we want to be, isn't it? In close fellowship with Jesus. But John also knew that this intimacy with Jesus was conditional. He speaks it so clearly in 1 John 1: *"So we are lying if we say we have fellowship with God but go on living in spiritual darkness; we are not practicing the truth."* To repent means to change our way of thinking from the wrong way to the right way. From our way to God's way. If we are going to walk this walk of intimacy with Jesus we need to walk it in the light and that means any sin must be confessed and forsaken.

We need to remember the price Jesus had to pay to deal with our sin. He doesn't want us to make excuses about it, dismiss it as bad habits or ignore it because sin carried such a high price tag. Our sin cost Jesus His life on the cross:

> *He was wounded for our transgressions,*
> *He was bruised for our iniquities;*
> *The chastisement for our peace was upon Him,*
> *And by His stripes we are healed.*
> *All we like sheep have gone astray;*
> *We have turned, every one, to his own way;*
> *And the Lord has laid on Him the iniquity of us all.*

(Isaiah 53:5,6 NKJV)

"How marvellous! How wonderful! Is my Saviour's love for me!" Don't turn away from that love, run to that love in confession of sin and receiving of His tremendous forgiveness. I don't want us to fall into the danger of being sin focussed however. Our

relationship with Jesus is first and foremost a love relationship. Ask Him to keep your heart tender towards Him. When our focus is on loving Jesus we will quickly deal with anything that becomes a hindrance to that relationship.

Dove eyed. Because of the narrow shape of their head, doves are only able to focus on one object at a time. So a dove always has a singular focus. We all know what a **"two-timer"** is: someone who tries to juggle two loves at the same time. Perhaps they are attempting to maintain a home and family, giving the appearance that all is well, while at the same time carrying on an illicit affair. The Bible uses this picture of adultery to describe spiritual unfaithfulness to Jesus. Jesus has not only the right to be entitled to our first love, but He demands to be our only love. Listen to what the Bible says to those who "two-time" Him: *"You adulterers! Don't you realize that friendship with the world makes you an enemy of God? I say it again: If you want to be a friend of the world, you make yourself an enemy of God."* (James 4:4)

We need to make it clear here that when the Bible is talking about the world it doesn't mean the environment around about us where we live. This is not an excuse to cut ourselves off from everyone and everything. We need to remember that Jesus was the friend of sinners and often eat and drank with them. When the Bible talks about believers having an affair with the world, it is using the term world to describe an evil system headed by Satan that opposes God and leaves Him out. James isn't teaching us "*Don't be in the world*." He's saying, "*Don't be conformed to the world*"(see Romans 12:1-2). In other words, don't go and have a relationship with the world that Jesus can't be a part of.

Right throughout the Bible, a dove is symbolic of the Holy Spirit. Jesus taught us that when the Spirit came in all of His fullness He would lead us into all truth. Remember that Jesus had already made it clear to the disciples that He is truth (John 14:6). God's Holy Spirit has only one point of focus and that is Jesus Christ. It is Jesus that the Holy Spirit in us sees, sings about, longs for and leads us to worship. Not only is Jesus the singular focus of the Spirit, but also He is the singular focus of His Bride, who also has dove's eyes.

The Bride: *"Behold, you are fair, my love! Behold, you are fair! You have dove's eyes."* (Song of Solomon 1:15)

The Groom: *"His eyes are like doves, By the rivers of waters, Washed with milk,"* (Song of Solomon 5:12 NKJV)

Can I ask you gently, *"Is your heart divided between Jesus and the World? Where is your focus?"* Only you can answer that. May I suggest that you get alone with Jesus and prayerfully read through James 4:1-10. Ask the Holy Spirit to show you how your love life with Jesus is doing.

Remember this:

Jesus Christ so wanted to have a love relationship with you that he pursued you for it! Think of the lengths that Jesus went to enable you to enter into intimacy with Him. Still yourself before God and read the following words thoughtfully and prayerfully. As we saw in Chapter 2, ask Jesus to open the Scriptures and to open your mind to understand what Jesus did for you that you might know Him intimately.

And they went out to a place called Golgotha (which means "Place of the Skull"). The soldiers gave Jesus wine mixed with bitter gall, but when he had tasted it, he refused to drink it. After they had nailed him to the cross, the soldiers gambled for his clothes by throwing dice. Then they sat around and kept guard as he hung there. A sign was fastened above Jesus' head, announcing the charge against him. It read: *"This is Jesus, the King of the Jews."* Two revolutionaries were crucified with him, one on his right and one on his left. The people passing by shouted abuse, shaking their heads in mockery. *"Look at you now!"* they yelled at him. *"You said you were going to destroy the Temple and rebuild it in three days. Well then, if you are the Son of God, save yourself and come down from the cross!"* The leading priests, the teachers of religious law, and the elders also mocked Jesus. *"He saved others,"* they scoffed, *"but he can't save himself! So he is the King of Israel, is he? Let him come down from the cross right now, and we will believe in him! He trusted God, so let God rescue him now if he wants him! For he said, 'I am the Son of God.'"* Even the revolutionaries who were crucified with him ridiculed him in the same way.

At noon, darkness fell across the whole land until three o'clock. At about three o'clock, Jesus called out with a loud voice, *"Eli, Eli, lama sabachthani?"* which means *"My God, my God, why have you abandoned me?"*

Some of the bystanders misunderstood and thought he was calling for the prophet Elijah. One of them ran and filled a sponge with sour wine, holding it up to him on a reed stick so he could drink. But the rest said, *"Wait! Let's see whether Elijah comes to save him."*

Then Jesus shouted out again, and he released his spirit. At that moment the curtain in the sanctuary of the Temple was torn in two, from top to bottom. The earth shook, rocks split apart, and tombs opened. The bodies of many godly men and women who had died were raised from the dead. They left the cemetery after Jesus' resurrection, went into the holy city of Jerusalem, and appeared to many people.

The Roman officer and the other soldiers at the crucifixion were terrified by the earthquake and all that had happened. They said, *"This man truly was the Son of God!"* (Matthew 27)

For God made Christ, who never sinned, to be the offering for our sin, so that we could be made right with God through Christ. (2 Corinthians 5:21)

Live a life filled with love, following the example of Christ. He loved us[a] and offered himself as a sacrifice for us, a pleasing aroma to God. (Ephesians 5:2)

You were created in the image of God. You were created good. Sin marred and destroyed that image. Jesus is your Rescuer, He came to bring you back to that image. Paul states, **"It doesn't matter whether we have been circumcised or not. What counts is whether we have been transformed into a new** *creation.*" (Galatians 6:15) He died that you might live.

Worship that expresses itself in adoration – (Praise & Prayer)

One of the many amazing things that I have learnt over the past ten years is to give myself in the worship of Jesus. David danced before the Lord with all his might and he only had a limited understanding under the old covenant of who God was. How much more should we, who have the privilege of the finished work of the cross and the full revelation of the Bible and the indwelling of the Spirit worship and adore our wonderful Saviour? Shouldn't our worship be energetic, enthusiastic and exuberant? Jesus truly is worthy of all glory and honour and praise. When we sing praise to Jesus, He deserves that we do so with all of our heart, mind, soul and strength. You're very being poured out in a praise sacrifice for who He is, what He has done, is doing and will do in days to come. As someone who had no great musical talent, I love the emphasis of the Psalmist on the fact that we can shout to the Lord and make a joyful noise. As beautiful as good music and singing are the emphasis ought to be on the expression of our heart and the focus always on the one we are worshiping.

Worship that expresses itself in active service – (Working & Witnessing)

If you are passionately in love with someone the natural thing is that you want to do things for them and you tell others about them. The Apostle Paul put it this way, *"For the love of Christ compels us..."* (2 Cor.5:14) The response that we make to the love of Jesus shown towards us is to love Him back and to demonstrate that love by serving Him and telling others about Him. Don't just tell Jesus you love Him, demonstrate that love by how you live your life.

An old sermon illustration that makes me smile goes like this: The young boy sent the following love note to his girlfriend.

My dearest Sally,

> *I love you more than anything else in the whole world. I would climb the highest mountain just to be with you. I would walk across the hottest desert just to be with you. I would swim the deepest ocean just to be with you. Nothing can separate us and our love.*

Your beloved Michael.

P.S. See you Saturday night if it does not rain.

May we not worship in words that turn out to be meaningless, but in love that leads to action.

Such love, pure as the whitest snow
Such love, weeps for the shame I know
Such love, paying the debt I owe
O Jesus, such love

See from His head, His hands, His feet,
Sorrow and love flow mingled down!
Did e'er such love and sorrow meet,
Or thorns compose so rich a crown?

Were the whole realm of nature mine,
That were a present far too small;
Love so amazing, so divine,
Demands my soul, my life, my all.

Four

Silence & Solitude – Listening to Jesus.

"It is important that we get still to wait on God. And it is best that we get alone, preferably with our Bible outspread before us. Then if we will we may draw near to God and begin to hear Him speak to us in our hearts"
A.W. Tozer

There is one condition for hearing the voice of Jesus. Jesus makes it so clear to us – *"My sheep hear my voice, and I know them, and they follow me:"* (John 10:27). The question is then, **"Are we His sheep?"** This is a crucial issue to get clear. If we do not know Jesus as our personal Lord and Saviour, then we will not be able to hear His voice, no matter how hard we try. If we do know Jesus as our Rescuer from sin, our Saviour from the fall, then this is a tremendous privilege and blessing. We can expect to hear His voice not because of anything that we have done, but because of what Jesus has done for us. Perhaps we should take a few moments just to thank Him for our so great salvation.

Jesus will never force Himself upon us, we must desire and seek to hear His voice. As the prophet Jeremiah stated, *"If you look for me wholeheartedly, you will find me."* (29:13) If we are content to live without hearing the voice of Jesus, then we will. But when we determine that we are going to hear the voice of Jesus then we will. If there is a problem in hearing the voice of Jesus, the problem is not on His behalf. The problem is on our side, it is a hearing problem, not a speaking problem.

God instructs us in Proverbs 4:20 *"**My child, pay attention to what I say. Listen carefully to my words.**"* Pay attention, listen carefully. My dog can appear to be lying in a deep sleep, dead to the world, but the next second his ears are cocked, and his head is turned to one side. Something has caught his attention and he is listening. That needs to be our attitude towards Jesus.

Jesus speaking in Matthew 13:15 says, *"**For the hearts of this people have grown dull. Their ears are hard of hearing,**"* How easy it is for our ears to get hard of hearing towards the voice of Jesus. Jesus is speaking but are we listening? We need to tune our ears and our heart towards the voice of Jesus.

It is easy to fall into the misconception that if only we had been alive when Jesus was, how wonderful it would have been to have sat down and had a chat with Him. As excellent as that would have been it runs contrary to what Jesus taught in John Chapter 16. Listen to the words of Jesus - *"But in fact, it is best for you that I go away, because if I don't, the Advocate* (The Holy Spirit, the Spirit of Christ) *won't come. If I do go away, then I will send him to you.... When the Spirit of truth comes, he will guide you into all truth. He will not speak on his own but will tell you what he has heard. He will tell you about the future. He will bring me glory by telling you whatever he receives from me."* Jesus is speaking to the Disciples, those who had been with Him day and night for three years and He says to them, it is best for you that I go away. If we get nothing else from this book, is there any way that we possibly can grasp this:

According to Jesus, we are in a better position today, having the Holy Spirit, than the disciples were when Jesus walked and talked with them.

Why then would the majority of those who call themselves sheep, followers of Jesus, find themselves struggling with hearing the voice of

Jesus as their normal experience?

In 1 Kings 19:2 we find that God spoke to Elijah in a *"still small voice."* It is so easy for the clutter, clamour and noise of this world to drown out the quiet speaking voice of Jesus. We are definitely living in **"the time of the end, when many will rush here and there, and knowledge will increase."** As described by Daniel. Busy, busy, busy certainly describes life for most people. I like this sermon illustration and pray that it will give you some food for thought.

Satan called a worldwide convention of demons. In

his opening address he said,

"We can't keep Christians from going to church. We can't keep them from reading their Bibles and knowing the truth.

We can't even keep them from forming an intimate relationship with their Saviour. Once they gain that connection with Jesus, our power over them is broken."

"So let them go to their churches; let them have all their programs and activities, BUT steal their time, so they don't have time to develop a relationship with Jesus Christ."

"This is what I want you to do," said the devil:

"Distract them from gaining hold of their Saviour and maintaining that vital connection throughout their day!"

"How shall we do this?" his demons shouted.

"Keep them busy in the non-essentials of life and invent innumerable schemes to occupy their minds," he answered.

"Tempt them to spend, spend, spend, and borrow, borrow, borrow. Persuade the wives to go to work for long hours and the husbands to work 6-7 days each week, 10-12 hours a day, so they can afford their empty lifestyles."

"Keep them from spending time with their children."

"As their families fragment, soon, their homes will offer no escape from the pressures of work!"

"Over-stimulate their minds so that they cannot hear that still, small voice."

"Entice them to play music constantly."

"To keep the TV and computers on, internet streaming constantly, and see to it that every shop and restaurant in the world plays non-biblical music constantly."

"This will jam their minds and break that union with

Christ. Fill the coffee tables with magazines and newspapers. Pound their minds with the news 24 hours a day. Invade their driving moments with advertising. Flood their mailboxes with junk mail, mail order catalogues, lotteries, and every kind of newsletter and promotional offering free products, services and false hopes."

"Even in their recreation and sport, let them be excessive. Have them return from their recreation and holidays exhausted."

"Keep them too busy to go out in nature and reflect on God's creation. Send them to amusement parks, sporting events, plays, concerts, and movies instead. Keep them busy, busy, busy!"

"And when they meet for spiritual fellowship, involve them in gossip and small talk so that they leave with troubled consciences."

"Crowd their lives with so many good causes they have no time to seek power from Jesus. Soon they will be working in their own strength, sacrificing their health and family for the good of the cause."

"It will work!" "It will work!"

It was quite a plan!

The demons went eagerly to their assignments causing Christians everywhere to get busier and more rushed, going here and there. Having little time for their God or their families. Having no time to tell others about the power of Jesus to change lives.

I guess the question is, has the devil been successful in his schemes?

You be the judge ... does "**BUSY**" mean:

B-eing

U-nder

S-atan's

Y-oke?

In Mark chapter four Jesus states, *"The seed that fell among the thorns represents others who hear God's word, but all too quickly the message is crowded out by the worries of this life, the lure of wealth, and the desire for other things, so no fruit is produced."* What is the answer? We need to UNPLUG from so many of the things that distract us from hearing the voice of Jesus. God makes it so clear to us in Psalm 46:10 – *"**Be still, and know that I am God!**"* Not just physically still, though to sit still is good. But to still our mind, to still our thoughts, to be still from all the distractions. We live in a day and age when being busy and the ability to multitask is viewed as a commendable quality. In the chaos of the digital age, it's easier than ever before to *"gain the whole world, and yet lose your soul."* Perhaps God is calling you to dial your life right down to a place of stillness. Instead of being wound up, wind down.

Take a few minutes to ponder upon these verses:

"Let all that I am wait quietly before God, for my hope is in him.

He alone is my rock and my salvation, my fortress where I will not be shaken.

My victory and honour come from God alone.

He is my refuge, a rock where no enemy can reach me.

O my people, trust in him at all times.

Pour out your heart to him, for God is our refuge." (Psalm 62:5-8)

"Be silent before the Lord, all humanity, for he is springing into action from his holy dwelling." (Zechariah 2:13)

"But the Lord is in his holy Temple. Let all the earth be silent before him." (Habakkuk 2:20)

When I was at Bible College we had a godly lecturer called Pastor Hardie. Pastor Hardie was dying from a terminal illness and by the end of the lecture he used to be soaked in sweat and exhausted. Often he looked at us young students and made this comment –

"God's two best friends are silence and solitude. For it is in the silence we hear His voice and in the solitude we feel His presence."

This was the example of Jesus. Jesus began His public ministry with 40 days of withdrawal into the desert wilderness to fast and pray in solitude and silence. His time alone with the Father empowered him to resist Satan's temptations and it focused and prepared him for his public ministry. Right throughout Jesus' ministry of preaching, healing, and teaching we see him withdraw from the crowds again and again – often getting up very early to do so – in order to be quiet and alone with the Father. There are many examples in the Gospels of Jesus' Solitude and Silence with the Father and how important it was to him.

Jesus taught his disciples to follow his prayer practice. *"Then Jesus said, "Let's go off by ourselves to a* quiet place and rest awhile." He said this because there were so many people coming and going that Jesus and his apostles didn't even have time to eat." (Mark 6:31-32) The Apostle Paul knew very well the importance of silence and solitude. After his encounter with the risen Christ he spent three days in solitude and silence for prayer and fasting (Acts 9:9). Then after being ministered to by Ananias and visiting with the disciples he withdrew to commune with Christ for three years in the isolation of the Arabian Desert. (Galatians 1:15-16)

"The purpose of silence and solitude," says Richard Foster, "is to be able to see and hear" (Celebration of Discipline, p. 86). The Spirit speaks to us when our heart is still and silent before the Lord – not when we're rushing about and doing our own thing in our own way.

When we're deeply in love with someone we think about them when we get up in the morning and when we go to sleep at night — we think of them all the time! Spend extended time with Jesus in solitude and silence and you will grow more and more in love with him!

Steps to stillness

Thankfully, we don't need to become monks living in private huts in the desert to practice the disciplines of solitude and silence! We do need to create a place of sanctuary. This can be a place in isolated nature, a spot by the river bank, a chair in a quiet room, somewhere we can be in peace.

You can walk, sit, kneel, lie down, it doesn't really matter though lying on your bed might mean that you just fall asleep.

It may be helpful to read a hymn or a psalm meditating on the words and meaning. Focus your attention on Him through praise and worship. Submit yourself and your circumstances into the hands of God. Most of us are familiar with the prayer that Jesus prayed during His darkest trial in the Garden of Gethsemane. *"Not as I will, but as You will."* Resign and rest in God's will. Quiet your spirit before Jesus and in faith ask Him to speak to you.

It is of great value to from time to time, set aside a day or longer for a retreat with Jesus at a quiet place that you can be left alone for long periods of time. Think of this as spending time alone with Jesus, doing something that you want to do with your Best Friend, something that will renew your soul!

Dietrich Bonhoeffer believed that solitude was so valuable in helping him to listen to God's Word and center his mind on God that he practiced it at the start and end of every day: "*We are silent at the beginning of the day because God should have the first word, and we are silent before going to sleep because the last word also belongs to God... Silence is nothing else but waiting for God's Word and coming from God's Word with a blessing. But everybody knows that this is something that needs to be practiced and learned*" (Life Together, p. 79).

If you are really struggling to control your thoughts and get quiet with Jesus it might be of benefit to try journaling. A journal can be a document on your computer, or just a good old-fashioned notebook. It can have long entries or short ones. It can be a place for recording God's blessings, peeling at the layers of your own heart, writing out prayers, meditating on Scripture, and dreaming about the future. God told Habakkuk to record the vision (Hab. 2:2). This was not an isolated command. The Scriptures record many examples of individual's prayers and God's replies (e.g. the Psalms, many of the prophets, Revelation). Just jot down what comes to mind. Don't try to analysis it or dissect it, you can read over it later and do that, taking time to test and examine it carefully, to make sure that it lines up with Scripture (1 Thess. 5:21).

Sit back comfortably, take out your pen and paper (or computer or iPad), smile, and turn your attention toward the Lord in praise and worship, seeking His face. Write down, *"Good morning, Lord! I love You."* Then become still, fixing the eyes of your heart by faith on Jesus. As thoughts come to mind simply write them down.

> **"Let the peace that comes from Christ rule in your hearts."** (Colossians 3:15)

Five

Speaking in the Spirit – Language of intimacy.

We have many Christian clichés that so easily roll off our tongue. It's not about religion, it's about a personal relationship. Christianity is not going to Church it is a living real friendship with Jesus. However the question I would like to ask you over a cup of coffee is this. *"Friend, you say you have a personal relationship with Jesus, please tell me how you speak with Him?"*

We have been thinking of how Jesus speaks to us when we listen, but when last did you speak to Him? *"Andrew"* you might say, *"all the time when I pray"*! Good, but I think that we need to pause and analysis our prayer language. Is what we call prayer really the way that we would talk with a good friend, with our best friend?

In this age of electronic communication, there is still nothing like spending time with a friend in person. When we are able to speak face to face, we can grasp a person's emotions and feelings. We see this face-to-face relationship between the Lord and Moses, the man God chose to deliver His people. Moses grew in his relationship with God as He walked with Him despite the rebellion and idolatry of the people. After the people worshipped the golden calf instead of God (Exodus 32), Moses set up a tent outside of the camp to meet with God while the people watched from a distance. As the pillar of cloud symbolizing God's presence descended to the tent, Moses spoke on their behalf to God. *"Inside the Tent of Meeting, the Lord would speak to Moses face to face, as one speaks to a friend."* (Exodus 33:11)

Because of the death of Jesus on the cross and His resurrection, we no longer need someone like Moses to speak with God for us. Instead, just as Jesus offered to His disciples, we can have a friendship with God through Christ. *"I no longer call you slaves, because a master doesn't confide in his slaves. Now you are my friends, since I have told you everything the Father told me."* (John 15:15). We need this truth to penetrate deep into our heart and soul. We are not like Moses. Moses lived and operated under the Old Covenant. Any relationship that Moses had with God we can have and so much more. Jesus taught us this truth about John the Baptist that he was *"of all who have ever lived, none is greater than John the Baptist."* John the Baptist was the greatest of the Old Covenant, but Jesus didn't stop there. He went on to say, *"Yet even the least person in the Kingdom of Heaven is greater than he is!"* Who are these people who are in the Kingdom of Heaven? Listen again to Jesus in John Chapter 3 - *"I assure you, no one can enter the Kingdom of God without being born of water and the Spirit. Humans can reproduce only human life, but the Holy Spirit gives birth to spiritual life. So don't be surprised when I say, 'You must be born again.'"* Can we grasp this awesome reality; if you are born again of the Spirit of God, then you have entered into the Kingdom of God, and even if you are the least in that Kingdom then you are still greater in privilege and position than the greatest of the Old Testament saints?

When we are born again our relationship with Jesus goes much deeper than friendship. The apostle Paul paints this picture in 2 Corinthians: *"For I am jealous for you with godly jealousy. For I have betrothed you to one husband, that I may present you as a chaste virgin to Christ."* Here he is teaching that we are betrothed to Jesus. The New Testament calls

Jesus the 'bridegroom' and the church 'his bride.' To understand what this means is life-changing. We need to understand this in the context of Jewish marriage in Bible times. The different aspects of first-century Jewish marriages each shed light on the New Testament's understanding of our relationship with Jesus.

Biblical marriage began with the betrothal and this was considered as binding as marriage. A woman who was betrothed was considered the "wife" of the man she was betrothed to, and she was bound to be faithful. The man initiated the process by pledging his life to his potential bride on the condition that she will accept his offer and return his love and pledge. The birth, life, death and resurrection of Jesus is God's proposal of love toward us. The amazing thing is that God did this when we had no interest or desire for Him. *"But God showed his great love for us by sending Christ to die for us while we were still sinners."* (Romans 5:8) God made the ultimate sacrifice upfront, He took the initiative, seeking to win the heart of His potential bride. The so great salvation that is offered to us through Jesus is God's invitation to join Him at the *"Marriage supper of the lamb."*

It takes two to make a marriage and the betrothal was only entered into when the prospective bride accepted the invitation and pledged her life to the groom. We see this in the Genesis account of Isaac and Rebekah. Abraham had sent his servant to find a wife for his son Isaac. The servant had discussed the proposal with Rebekah's family but then she was consulted. *"Well,"* they said, *"we'll call Rebekah and ask her what she thinks."* So they called Rebekah. *"Are you willing to go with this man?"* they asked her. And she replied, *"Yes, I will go."* (Genesis 24:57) God doesn't want to force salvation on us, He wants us to freely choose to love Him in response to His loving sacrifice for us. ***"We love Him because He first loved us."*** (1 John 4:19 NKJV) We enter into this relationship with our heavenly bridegroom the moment we say **"yes"** to His proposal, pledging to return His love and to surrender our life's over to Him.

The proposal and its acceptance were followed by a public announcement. Almost all covenants in the Bible begin with a public ceremony and this was also true of biblical marriages. While a full wedding ceremony wouldn't take place for some time, it was expected that the couple would publicly declare their covenant pledges in a betrothal ceremony soon after the woman accepted the proposal. This is one of the many reasons why I believe that water baptism is so important. Through baptism, a person is publicly declaring their faith in Jesus and promising to live as a faithful covenant partner within the community of God's united bride, the Church.

In Bible times, couples were betrothed to one another for one or more years before they had a wedding ceremony and consummated their marriage. The betrothal period was a time when the bride and groom were able to prepare themselves for the life they were going to soon share together. The husband often went away and prepared a home for the future family while the woman would engage in practices that prepared her for her future life as a wife and mother. Jesus' parable about the virgins who hadn't prepared themselves for the returning bridegroom illustrates this period. This is the time that we are living in now while Jesus prepares a place that Paul describes as *"No eye has seen, no ear has heard, and no mind has imagined what God has prepared for those who love him."* (1Corinthians 2:9) The Bridegroom, Jesus, doesn't specify the day or time when he will be coming back for his bride. In fact, He tells his disciples plainly that He doesn't know when the Father will give His permission for the Son to come and gather us up and take us home. *"Only the Father knows"* (Matthew 24:36).

It was also customary for the groom to declare the seriousness of his pledge to his newly betrothed bride by giving her a precious gift. It was the bride's assurance while her groom was away that he would indeed return for her. Jesus gives us the precious betrothal gift of the Holy Spirit (We read about this in John 16). Jesus knows we cannot prepare ourselves for His return on our own, so He places His own Spirit inside of us to empower us and teach us how to live as we ought. He also doesn't want us to feel abandoned or distressed in his absence, so he gives us *"the Comforter"* (John 16:7) who is the assurance of our future inheritance in Christ (Ephesians 1:14).

These steps all lead up to the consummation of the marriage. When the home was prepared and the bride had made herself ready, the groom would return for his bride. The whole community would engage in a great wedding celebration and the couple would consummate their marriage and become "one flesh." After witnessing a vision portraying Gods' complete victory, John heard a multitude proclaiming: *"Praise the Lord! For the Lord our God, the Almighty, reigns. Let us be glad and rejoice, and let us give honour to him. For the time has come for the wedding feast of the Lamb, and his bride has prepared herself."* Then the angel said, *"Write this: Blessed are*

those who are invited to the wedding feast of the Lamb."
(Revelation 19:6-7, 9)

How awesome will that be when we join in the great wedding feast in Heaven?

There is coming a day when no heartaches shall come
No more clouds in the sky, no more tears to dim the eye.
All is peace forevermore on that happy golden shore,
What a day, glorious day that will be.

What a day that will be when my Jesus I shall see,
And I look upon His face,
The One who saved me by His grace;
When He takes me by the hand
And leads me through the Promised Land,
What a day, glorious day that will be.

There'll be no sorrow there,
No more burdens to bear,
No more sickness, no pain,
No more parting over there;
And forever I will be,
With the One who died for me,
What a day, glorious day that will be.

The death and resurrection of Jesus Christ changed everything. The Old Testament saints looked forward in faith. Those who walked with Jesus experienced the coming of the Kingdom. Now we can enter into the Kingdom. Jesus disciples went from being followers to friends. After the resurrection, the language changed again. When the woman encountered the risen Jesus in the garden it is very interesting how He described His disciples. Listen to what He said, *"Jesus met them and greeted them. And they ran to him, grasped his feet, and worshiped him. Then Jesus said to them, "Don't be afraid! Go tell my brothers to leave for Galilee, and they will see me there."* (Matthew 28:9,10) When Mary Magdalene met Jesus alive from the dead she grabbed hold of Him and Jesus gently rebuked her, *"Don't cling to me,"* Jesus said, *"for I haven't yet ascended to the Father. But go find my brothers and tell them, 'I am ascending to my Father and your Father, to my God and your God.'"* (John 20:17) Before the cross Jesus had told the disciples that they weren't servants but friends. Now He is calling them brothers. Now He is saying to Mary, *'I am ascending to my Father and your Father.'* Because of the death and resurrection of Jesus, we can enter into the family of God. He is our Father. Jesus is our brother, we are as Paul puts it - *"The Spirit Himself bears witness with our spirit that we are children of God, and if children, then heirs—heirs of God and joint heirs with Christ,"* (Romans 8:16,17) By faith we enter the family of God and become a brother of Jesus, a joint inheritor of all His blessings.

Friend, Fiancée, Family.

What beautiful pictures of the place and position of intimacy that we have with Jesus. All of this takes us back to the question of this chapter. If we find ourselves in this state of intimacy with Jesus, then surely our prayer language must reflect this. I ask myself this question as I ask you -

"Do I talk to Jesus in the way that I would talk to my closest friend and dearest family member?"

The danger is that we have learned a mechanical and false way of praying that we feel we must repeat. Instead of focussing on the wrong way take some time out to ponder how you speak with a trusted loved one and then ask yourself how can you replicate that style of conversation in your prayer with Jesus? Check your conversation when you are praying. Pause and think about what and how you are speaking. Is it just vain repetition, or the same as placing an order, just a list of wants and wishes? How would it affect our human relationships if we spoke, or as the case may be, didn't speak in the same way as we pray? I believe that if we have the right view of our relationship with Jesus then the right form of speech will flow out of that true understanding.

I will pray with my mind – rational, reasoned response to what we are facing in our circumstances or to what Jesus has been saying to us. Engaging with focused thoughtfulness. Think about what you are praying!

I will pray with my spirit - an overflowing outpouring of love that comes from deep within and gushes out in adoration, worship, praise, an exaltation of Jesus Christ our Lord and Saviour. A response to God that is full of emotion. We do not need to be afraid of emotion. Paul teaches us in Romans 14:17 that *"the kingdom of God is not a matter of eating and drinking, but of righteousness, peace and joy in the Holy Spirit."* We can describe righteousness as doctrine and peace and joy as emotions. So yes our prayers must be doctrinal truth, but not cold and dry words, instead words that are fired with love and passion.

One last thought. Never forget that when you go to see a friend for a chat that it is more than a conversation that you are looking for, you are also looking to enjoy their presence. Tim Keller puts it like this, *"Prayer is both conversation and encounter with God. . . . We must know the awe of praising his glory, the intimacy of finding his grace, and the struggle of asking his help, all of which can lead us to know the spiritual reality of his presence."*

Face to face! O blissful moment!
Face to face—to see and know;
face to face with my Redeemer,
Jesus Christ who loves me so!

Carrie E. Breck

Live loved by Jesus

Six

Surrendering self – Leaving off the old man.

"…throw off your old sinful nature and your former way of life, which is corrupted by lust and deception. Instead, let the Spirit renew your thoughts and attitudes. Put on your new nature, created to be like God—truly righteous and holy."
Ephesians 4:22-24

Jesus Christ held nothing back for us and He will hold nothing back from us. He was completely broken and poured out for us on the cross. But in return the call comes clearly back to us – *"If any of you wants to be my follower, you must give up your own way, take up your cross, and follow me. If you try to hang on to your life, you will lose it. But if you give up your life for my sake, you will save it"* (Matthew 16:24,25).

Can we hear the call of Jesus?

GIVE UP YOUR LIFE FOR MY SAKE.

We speak of this as living the **"Surrendered life."** To surrender literally means to give up something to another person. It can also mean to give up or give back (something that has been granted). The surrendered life is the act of giving back to Jesus the life he granted you. It's relinquishing control, rights, power, direction, all the things you do and say. It's totally giving your life over to his hands, to do with you as he pleases.

Jesus is the greatest example of a surrendered life: *"For I have come down from heaven to do the will of God who sent me, not to do my own will."* (John 6:38) *"I do not seek My own glory"* (8:50).

Jesus never did anything on his own initiative. His every action and every word reflected the Father. *"I do nothing on My own, but speak exactly what the Father has taught Me. ... I always do what pleases Him."* (8:28-29).

Jesus spoke these words as a flesh-and-blood man. Remember, He came to earth to live not as God but as a human being. He experienced life the way we do. And, like us, He had a will of his own, but Jesus chose to surrender that will to the Father fully; *"The reason the Father loves Me is that I lay down My life in order to take it up again. No one takes it from Me, but I lay it down of My own accord. I have authority to lay it down and authority to take it up again."* (10:17-18).

The call that comes to you and me is the same. Our loving Heavenly Father forces no-one to give up their lives to Him, but allows us the freedom and privilege to choose to give our lives to Him.

The apostle Paul choose to follow Jesus' example and life a fully surrendered life. Think of Paul's background! Paul was well educated, having been trained by the best teachers of his time. And he was a Pharisee, among the most zealous of all Jewish religious leaders. Paul had been a Jesus-hater, a self-righteous persecutor of Christians. He said he literally breathed hatred toward Christ's followers. Paul was on a career path right to the top of his religious organization.

However, God took this self-made, self-determined, self-directed man, and made him a shining example of the surrendered life. Paul became one of the most God-dependent, God-filled, God-led people in all of history. Paul's life became a blueprint for all who choose the fully surrendered life. This is how he put it; *"But God had mercy on me so that Christ Jesus could use me as a prime example of his great patience with even the worst sinners. Then others will realize that they, too, can believe in him and receive eternal life."* (1 Timothy 1:16)

The surrendered life exchanges our self-righteousness for Christ's all-sufficiency.

God actually knocked Paul off his high horse (if he was on one) as he was going his self-confident way towards Damascus. A blinding light came from heaven and Paul was knocked to the ground, trembling and a voice spoke from heaven saying *"Saul! Saul! Why are you persecuting me?"* (Acts 9:4) Those words would have catapulted Paul back to an event from months before that had shaken him to the core and left him in turmoil. The stoning of Stephen must have had a profound effect upon his life. Paul had come face to face with a fully God-surrendered man. A man who was willing to die for his Saviour Jesus Christ. Paul had trained for years in the Hebrew Scriptures but Stephen, an unlearned man spoke God's Word with authority. Paul had a quest for knowledge but Stephen had the very power of heaven, even as he died. Paul knew about God but Stephen knew God.

On his knees in the dust of the road, Paul heard these words from heaven; *"I am Jesus, the one you are persecuting!"* (Acts 9:5) It was a supernatural revelation that turned Paul's world upside down.

He had spent years in education and study and doing good works but the whole time he was on the wrong road. It a moment he understood what it was that Stephen possessed. An intimate knowledge of Jesus through a revelation of the Holy Spirit. Trembling and astonished, Paul responded, *"Lord, what do You want me to do?"* Jesus said to him, *"Now get up and go into the city, and you will be told what you must do."* We will never surrender to a theology or a teaching but when we experience a supernatural revelatory encounter with Jesus Christ it will change our lives and our allegiance.

Here is the formerly arrogant, aggressor now struck blind being led by his friends into the city. We need to come to this place where all self is gone and we are completely dependent upon God. All boasting and pride are gone. The things that once were so important and precious are now counted as muck. It is now all about Jesus. When he asked, *"Lord, what would you have me to do?"* his heart was crying out, *"Jesus, how can I serve you? How can I know you and please you? Nothing else matters."*

I love the link between being filled with the Spirit and the scales falling from Paul's eyes. *"So Ananias went and found Saul. He laid his hands on him and said, "Brother Saul, the Lord Jesus, who appeared to you on the road, has sent me so that you might regain your sight and be filled with the Holy Spirit. Instantly something like scales fell from Saul's eyes, and he regained his sight. Then he got up and was baptized."* (Acts 9:17,18) The old is gone, buried in baptism, the new has come, risen with Christ. Instead of being full of self he is now spirit filled. The evidence of this surrendered, Spirit filled life, *"And immediately he began preaching about Jesus in the synagogues, saying, "He is indeed the Son of God!"* The apostle grew bolder with every sermon, *"Saul's preaching became more and more powerful, and the Jews in Damascus couldn't refute his proofs that Jesus was indeed the Messiah."* (Acts 9:20,22)

I was 20 years of age, single, living at home with my parents. The previous year I had dropped out of university and had spent the following 10 months in a variety of jobs. An old rusty Ford Fiesta that just about got me from A to B was my pride and joy. It was Easter Sunday evening and Dr Rex Mathie from South Africa was preaching from the depths of his heart. *"What right has anyone to hear the gospel twice when so many people in the world have never heard of Jesus in a way to be able to make a decision about Him? Who will go and tell the world about Jesus?"* Into that service and into my life the Spirit of God spoke loud and clear, *"Andrew will you go and tell?"* At the altar call at the end of that service, I ran to the front of that church building and with tears running down my face, brokenly surrendered my all to God. It was a very real encounter with God that changed my life and lead to me going to Bible College in the autumn of that year.

Get this, however, I often look back and ask myself this question, "*What did I have to surrender?*" I had no responsibilities and few possessions. Life was simple and straightforward. In hindsight, what seemed like a massive act of self-sacrifice at the time was another step in a youthful adventure. As life progresses with marriage, family and responsibilities it gets increasingly complex. This is why I am continually drawn back to the words of Paul when he declared *"**I die daily.**"*(1 Corinthians 15:31)

Surrendering self is essential in the Christian life. It can be a past experience of absolute surrender. This is often key in nailing our colours to the mast and declaring that following Jesus is our priority. This might take place at water baptism or an act of surrendering our will to God. The old chorus that has been popularised again in recent years puts it like this:

I have decided to follow Jesus;
Tho' none go with me, I still will follow,

The world behind me, the cross before me,
No turning back, no turning back.

Perhaps you have heard the expression that you need to burn your boats behind you. The concept of burning boats traces back to one of history's most inspiring leadership stories in 1519. Hernán Cortés led a large expedition consisting of 600 Spaniards, 16 or so horses, and 11 boats to Mexico. The goal: capture a magnificent treasure said to be held there. Upon arrival, Cortés made history by destroying his ships by burning them. This sent a clear message to his men: There is no turning back. They either win or they perish. You might assume that Cortés' men would have become despondent, with no exit strategy in place to save their lives, they instead rallied behind their leader as never before. Within two years, he succeeded in his conquest of the Aztec empire.

At its essence, burning boats represents a point of no return, a mental commitment where you recognize that you have crossed a line never to cross back. There is no hedging, no looking over your shoulder. Everything now — all thoughts and efforts — must be focused on succeeding in this new reality. Hebrew tradition teaches a similar value. In ancient times, Israelite armies would besiege enemy cities from three sides only, leaving open the possibility of flight. They understood that so long as the enemy saw that they had an escape route available, they would not fight with utmost earnestness and energy.

In most cases, this played right into the besiegers' hands. When we make that decision to follow Jesus, from that point on our total focus needs to be fixed on Jesus, no looking back, no turning back, no looking for other options or escape routes, burn every boat behind you and press forward. Never look back.

When we come to that place of absolute surrender we are placing ourselves into the position that Colossians 3:1-3 teaches: *"If then you were raised with Christ, seek those things which are above, where Christ is, sitting at the right hand of God. Set your mind on things above, not on things on the earth. For you died, and your life is hidden with Christ in God. When Christ who is our life appears, then you also will appear with Him in glory."* (NKJV) We have died. That is our present position.

What a picture of intimacy for the child of God. J. B. Lightfoot, was an English theologian, preacher, canon of St Paul's Cathedral, and bishop of

Durham. This is his comment on being hidden with Christ. *"The apostle's argument is this: `When you sank under the baptismal water, you disappeared forever to the world. You rose again, it is true, but you rose only to God. The world henceforth knows nothing of your life, and (as a consequence) your new life must know nothing of the world."*

Practically we have to work this out. Paul said I die daily. The big question is how do we do this? The answer is by continually reckoning ourselves dead to self and alive to God. Whenever you face any temptation consider yourself dead to sin and alive to God in Christ. Believe that no matter how strong that temptation feels, Jesus broke its power on the Cross. Believe that by the Spirit's power, through faith, you can be dead to that sin. Believe that Christ did everything you need in order to put that sin to death and be fully alive to God. This does not mean I don't need to battle sin. But it means Christ has done everything necessary so that I can, by the Spirit's power, conquer every sin I face.

The important point to grasp is that we are always looking to Jesus and what He has done for us, and not looking at ourselves and what we are doing. We have to come to an understanding of our true position and identity in Christ. It is not working or trying harder. That will only lead to a restrictive legalism that more than often leaves us frustrated and downcast. Remember it is the truth that sets us free. When we live in the love of God, we live in freedom.

There is a positive cycle of change happening here. The more we reckon ourselves dead to self and the more we see ourselves alive in Christ the more intimate we become with Jesus. The more intimate we are with Jesus the easier it is to reckon ourselves dead to self and sin. The change is spiritual, it is supernatural it is not because of us it is all because of Jesus. It is not our trying harder through gritted teeth it is instead us resting in what Jesus has done for us. It is not works, it is grace.

All to Jesus I surrender,
All to Him I freely give;
I will ever love and trust Him,
In His presence daily live.

I surrender all,
I surrender all;
All to Thee, my blessed Saviour,
I surrender all.

All to Jesus I surrender,
Humbly at His feet I bow;

Worldly pleasures all forsaken,
Take me, Jesus, take me now.

All to Jesus I surrender,
Make me, Saviour, wholly Thine;
Let me feel the Holy Spirit,
Truly know that Thou art mine.

All to Jesus I surrender,
Lord, I give myself to Thee;
Fill me with Thy love and power,
Let Thy blessing fall on me.

All to Jesus I surrender,
Now I feel the sacred flame;
Oh, the joy of full salvation!
Glory, glory, to His Name!

Judson W. Van DeVenter, 1896

74 Rosses Lane
Ballymena
BT42 2SB
07718988839

Dear Friend,

The vision - In the spring of 2018 God deeply impressed upon my heart the vision of starting a Fellowship in Ballycastle both to reach that needy town and then that it might evangelise back down through the Glens with the Gospel of Jesus Christ. After an interesting journey at the start of 2019 we as family found ourselves leaving the Faith Mission and in a step of faith beginning to work in the Ballycastle area under the umbrella of NewGround Ireland.

We decided in order to put a stake in the ground and allow people in the community to know who we are and what we were doing that we would start Sunday morning gatherings at a conference room at the Enterprise centre. Early on we felt burdened for a particular area of housing around the Altananam Park area and we have had some amazing openings and conversations in the area. At the end of the summer God opened up the way for us to have the use of the Gaelic speaking primary school which is right on the edge of the housing area that we have been concentrating on. Numerically we might be small but looking back over nearly a year many strategic contacts have been made and work on the ground accomplished that will bear fruit in time to come.

Moving Forward - We are excited about our Christmas outreach. We plan to visit the area of

ings were spent prayer walking in the community and amongst other things this clearly indicated to us that very few stir before midday. With this in mind we will not be meeting on a Sunday morning in the new year but rather plan to run an Alpha Style course on Sunday evenings beginning with some food at 5:30 pm

Family News - Joshua is working hard in year 12 with his GCSE exams this year. He has developed a love of mountain biking and has even dragged his Dad along on a few hair raising (if he had any) adventures. Bethany is nearly thirteen and loves her sport and all things connected with animals particularly dogs. Barbara has started a Child care course course at the local college and with some work experience alongside that, supporting me in our ministry and keeping the family functioning remains very busy.

We look forward with excitement to see what God will do in 2020. We deeply appreciate your prayers and support as we are co-labourers together for a mighty harvest in Jesus name. As the Apostle Paul wrote to the Philippians, *"...you have been my partners in spreading the Good News about Christ."*

Yours in Jesus name,

Andrew, Barbara, Joshua & Bethany.

Please accept a copy of my book 'Known by Jesus' which contains some thoughts God gave me as we have begun this adventure as a token of our gratefulness for your support of us in the work of God.

Seven

Secure in the Saviour – Lay hold of Jesus

Jesus at the center of it all
Jesus at the center of it all
From beginning to the end
It will always be, it's always been You
Jesus, Jesus

Resting in Jesus – Abiding –

It was coming towards the end of the summer holidays. Soon it would be back to school and the normality of the daily routine. For a last treat we redeemed some vouchers and headed off to a 5-star hotel for a one night special. After checking in and admiring our room we jumped into the swimming pool and I soon expended my energy playing with the children, above and below the water, and swimming lengths. I hauled myself up the pool ladder before collapsing into the luxurious hot tub. Relaxing back into the warm bubbling water I allowed it to completely cover me with just my face jutting out. What a blissful feeling, given over to the relaxing warmth. Can we picture ourselves relaxing completely and confidently into the warmth of the love of Jesus? Letting everything else go and abiding continually in Him.

Likening abiding in Jesus to relaxing entirely in a hot tub is a far from the perfect picture. The Bible tells us that not only are we in Jesus but that Jesus is in us. *"For you died to this life, and your real life is hidden with Christ in God."* (Colossians 3:3). The picture is more that I die and am submerged into Jesus so that it is no longer any of me, now it is all Jesus. When a believer goes under the water in baptism it is a picture of being wholly buried into Jesus. The old has gone and the new has come. It is looking at situations and making decisions not by what resources we have but by what resources Jesus has. Getting to the place where we do not just know these words or repeat these words but rest in believing faith in these words – *"For I can do everything through Christ, who gives me strength."* (Philippians 4:13)

After some time relaxing in that hot tub, I had to get out of its warmth and comfort. The opposite is true of our Christian faith. On the wall of our kitchen, we have a poster of one of our favourite Psalms number 91. It begins- *"He who dwells in the secret place of the Most High shall abide under the shadow of the Almighty."*

How clear and plain this is; it does not say those who visit, or dip in and out, NO; it says those that live in the presence of God; those who make the presence of God their dwelling place; those that abide there. This is the place of intimacy, dwelling with God.

Things that once were wild alarms
Cannot now disturb my rest,
Closed in everlasting arms,
Pillowed on His loving breast;
Oh, to lie forever here,
Doubt and care and self resign,
While He whispers in my ear
I am His, and He is mine;

We don't *"try"* to abide in Christ. If you are in Christ, then you already abide (live) in Christ. It is our place and our position. As a family, we live in County Antrim, Ireland. I don't wake up in the morning and think to myself; *"I must get to County Antrim."* I am already there because it is my dwelling place where I abide. Living in Jesus is not a work it is a location. It is not my striving and seeking to be a better Christian in my self-effort but resting completely and utterly on all that Jesus has already done for me. It is not even a mental effort or exercise it is a heart effort or exercise. It is literally a place of yielding completely to Jesus. Our heart absolutely surrenders and our mind follows in an understanding of all that Jesus has done for us. *"My old self has been crucified with Christ. It is no longer I who live, but Christ lives in me. So I live in this earthly body by trusting in the Son of God, who loved me and gave himself for me."* (Galatians 2:20) Grace comes upon you when you rest and trust God. Live a life of rest. Have this attitude and tell the Lord, *"I can do nothing of myself. I just rest in You Lord and I trust You."*

Use your imagination with me for a few minutes. You are walking by the harbour and you fall into conversation with an extremely wealthy man. He asks you to do him a favour. He is going sailing in a small dingy for a few days as a personal adventure and has forgotten to leave his watch safely at home. He asks you if you would look after his watch for him until he comes back. He then shows you that it is an extremely valuable '*Patek Philippe – Model 2523*' worth well over a million pounds and tells you that he will reward you with a half a million pounds if you return it to him undamaged but if you lose it you will need to replace the watch. He asks you to keep it in your pocket the whole time, not in a safe or some other secure location. You accept the assignment and carefully place the watch in your inner pocket. Now consider this, do you think that over the next few days that you would be conscious of the watch in your pocket? Do you think that you would be continually putting your hand over your pocket checking that it was there, that it would be continually on your mind or would it be very difficult for you to remember that you were carrying that expensive watch? I think that you would be very aware and always thinking of that watch in your possession. Now think of this. You carry something that is of greater value than the watch for which your reward will be out of this world. It is not work or effort for us to be conscious of the fact that Jesus is in us and we are in Him. Our focus and affection should naturally be fixed on Jesus.

1 Corinthians 6:17 – "**But the person who is joined to the Lord is one spirit with him.**" Joined to the Lord in one Spirit. Drawing from the one root.

You may have heard it said that you spell **FAITH** like this – **R.I.S.K.** and it is certainly true that we have to step out of our comfort zone and take risks in order to see God move. However, it is also true that you can spell **FAITH** like this – **T.R.U.S.T.** or perhaps like this **R.E.S.T.** The Holy Spirit manifests Himself when we are still. Stillness releases the supernatural when we wait upon the Lord – It is all about Jesus & not about ourselves.

Receiving from Jesus - Anointing

The blessed man of Psalm 1 is described like this, *"They are like trees planted along the riverbank, bearing fruit each season. Their leaves never wither, and they prosper in all they do."* For the Christian our roots should be continually growing deep into Jesus then we draw our spiritual life not from ourselves or externally but from Him alone.

We had a Eucalyptus tree growing in the corner of the garden. It had grown rapidly rising above the height of the house and swayed violently in the winter winds. It was time for it to go but I had a problem. The trunk of the tree was much too wide for my saw so I decided to prune it right down as far as I could go until I could borrow a larger saw. The result was a skeleton tree about ten feet tall, just the trunk and a few stubby branches left. Borrowing a saw and getting the tree cut right down was one of those jobs that I just never got around to. Spring came and something amazing began to happen. The tree might have looked dead but the root system was still intact and fully functioning. The roots began to push life giving sap up into the tree trunk and what appeared to be dead burst into life. Shoots pushed out all over that trunk and leaves began to appear. The life from the roots produced visible life on the surface. When we are rooted and grounded in Jesus, abiding in Him, we cannot but know His life flowing from us.

Jesus taught us this so clearly in John chapter 15, *"Remain in me, and I will remain in you. For a branch cannot produce fruit if it is severed from the vine, and you cannot be fruitful unless you remain in me. Yes, I am the vine; you are the branches. Those who remain in me, and I in them, will produce much fruit. For apart from me you can do nothing. Anyone who does not remain in me is thrown away like a useless branch and withers. Such branches are gathered into a pile to be burned. But if you remain in me and my words remain in you, you may ask for anything you want, and it will be granted! When you produce much fruit, you are my true disciples. This brings great glory to my Father. Remain in my love."*

This brings us full circle – if we want to be known by Jesus and be sure that we never hear those terrifying words, *"I never knew you!"* we need to be connected to Jesus. That, of course begins at salvation when we repent of our sinful life and turn in faith to Jesus, appropriating to ourselves all the benefits of the finished work of the cross. The Holy Spirit will constantly reveal the abundant love of Jesus unto us helping us to grasp the tremendous truth stated by Jesus in John Chapter 15:9 *"I have loved you even as the Father has loved me."* That's God's part. Then the verse goes on to tell us that all we have to do is, remain, continue, and abide in that love, safe and secure in the arms of Jesus. The little book of Jude instructs us similarly. *"But you, beloved, building yourselves up on your most holy faith, praying in the Holy Spirit, keep yourselves in the love of God, looking for the mercy of our Lord Jesus Christ unto eternal life."* (Jude 20,21 NKJV) As we abide in Jesus, we learn to know Him better and trust Him more.

As I penned these words it is full blown autumn weather. The leaves are coming off the trees like driven snow. This is caused by a complicated process called abscission. One of the components of this process is that the life producing sap that has been flowing from the roots of the tree begins to dry up. I was worshipping and meditating on this truth that all our spiritual life flows from Jesus indwelling us as we abide in Him and God spoke this powerful word into my heart. In Jesus there is no autumn or winter. The life that flows from Jesus never dries up or even slows down. Jesus proclaimed that He is the living water and whoever drinks shall never, never, never thirst again. The life keeps flowing and because of this we can keep on going.

A missionary in Africa several decades ago lived in a small hut which had electricity supplied by a quiet, small generator. The little diesel powered wonder supplied current for both his home and the simple church building beside it. Late one afternoon two African men from another much more remote village visited the Pastor in his hut, and were amazed when night fell, and he simply switched the room lights on. They were wide-eyed at the electric light bulb hanging from the ceiling of his living space. One of the visitors asked the Pastor if he could have one of the bulbs. Thinking perhaps he wanted it for a sort of trinket, the Pastor obliged and gave it to him. Months passed. On his next visit to the remote village of that same man, the Pastor stopped at the hut of the man who had previously asked for the bulb. Imagine his surprise when he saw the bulb hanging from an ordinary string. The man understood the general idea of connection, but he didn't understand that it needed to be plugged into the right power source.

The Key is connection to Jesus.

Paul puts it so plainly in 1 Corinthians 13. *"If I had the gift of prophecy, and if I understood all of God's secret plans and possessed all knowledge, and if I had such faith that I could move mountains, but didn't love others, I would be nothing...."* Seeking to do the work of God without the love of God will accomplish nothing. Romans 5:5 reminds us, *"For we know how dearly God loves us, because he has given us the Holy Spirit to fill our hearts with his love."* We come to experience the love of God at salvation. We allow God by His Spirit to fill our lives with His love. We abide and remain in that love. Everything that we seek to do must flow from that place of love. Three things will last forever--faith, hope, and love--and the greatest of these is love.

I bring these thoughts to a close with an illustration that made sense to me and that I hope will make sense to you as well. My daughter has the most beautiful long blonde hair. Whether it is watching it blow in the wind, shine as she brushes it or the silky feel as I get to stroke it during daddy daughter hugs it is a thing of beauty and gorgeous charm. However, it also falls to me from time to time to have the dubious privilege of removing matted clumps of the same hair from the U-bend of the bathroom sink. What was once a delight is now completely disgusting! What makes the difference? Connection! Without connection, what was once beautiful is now repulsive. Don't allow ugliness to creep into your life because of not having the proper deep rooted union with Jesus. Pursue intimacy and connection with Jesus so that you might shine with His beauty.

I've found a new way of living
I've a new life divine
I've got the fruit of the Spirit
I'm abiding, abiding in the vine

Abiding in the vine, Abiding in the vine
Love joy health peace
He has made them mine
I've got prosperity, power and victory
Abiding, abiding in the vine

CONCLUSION

Grow Deep to Go High.

The prophet Ezekiel describes the strength of the Assyrian Empire as a flourishing tree because of its well-watered roots. It was, *"like a cedar of Lebanon, with beautiful branches that cast deep forest shade and with its top high among the clouds. Deep springs watered it and helped it to grow tall and luxuriant. The water flowed around it like a river, streaming to all the trees nearby. This great tree towered high, higher than all the other trees around it. It prospered and grew long thick branches because of all the water at its roots. It was strong and beautiful, with wide-spreading branches, for its roots went deep into abundant water."* We need to go deep in intimacy with Jesus to allow us to go high and wide in power and authority. To know Him and to be known by Him. The prophet Daniel put it like this, *"the people who know their God shall be strong, and carry out great exploits."*

The inevitable consequence of pursuing a life of intimacy with Jesus is an overflowing that will impact the world around about us.

One evening at a house meeting I was sharing my heart's desire to see God move in revival power right across our island of Ireland. An elderly lady spoke up telling her memory of a message that Duncan Campbell gave at the Faith Mission Bangor Convention in 1964. God used Duncan Campbell in successive waves of revival throughout the Scottish Hebridean islands in the 1940s and 1950s. He described revival as a *"Community saturated with God."* He came to the Faith Mission Bible College in Scotland and spoke to the students while the Lewis Revival was still going on. He told of a midwife having a vision of Ireland all in darkness but then a light breaking out in the South that filled the whole land. In 1964 while preaching at a conference in Ireland, Mr. Campbell prophesied, Ireland will have riots and revival. In the light of this, he came aside to seek the face of God during which he received a vision of a coming revival to Ireland. He described how God would visit the island through small bands of praying people in the country districts. That evening after preaching his last message of the convention, God took over. The people were gripped with awe and no-one could move for the next half-an-hour during this divine stillness and quietness at least four people heard indescribable sounds from heaven. Then the people began to weep and pray.

Ireland was once known as the *'Land of Saints and Scholars,'* but today it has turned its back on God and has become a secular society. The cause is not a lost one, however. Ireland was held by the power of the Druids and paganism, but one man answered the call of God to come with the gospel message. He preached Jesus the length and breadth of the land in the power of the Holy Spirit with many signs following. The result, Ireland turned from paganism to Christianity in his life time. That man was, of course, Saint Patrick.

If we want to see God move in Supernatural power that will impact our communities and our countries, then we must pursue this quest for intimacy with Jesus.

Though this is the conclusion of this little book my prayer is that it will just be the beginning of a great adventure with God leading to a life of fruitfulness.

"It is a joy to Jesus when a person takes time to walk more intimately with Him. The bearing of fruit is always shown in Scripture to be a visible result of an intimate relationship with Jesus Christ"

Oswald Chambers

Living out the message that we have been speaking about will God willing be the subject of a follow-up book **– Known by the devil.**

About the Author

Andrew McIlroy has been involved in Christian ministry since his teenage years. He spent three years at the Faith Mission Bible College Edinburgh and has an earned Bachelor's and Master's Degree in Theology. Andrew has served as an evangelist with the Faith Mission as well as pastoring two churches and is presently involved in pioneering church planting right across Ireland. Although he has an interest in world mission, his primary passion is for the people of Ireland.

You can contact him or keep updated with his ministry by going to the following **Facebook page**:

Andrew & Barbara McIlroy

Or email: mcilroy.ireland@gmail.com

Printed in Poland
by Amazon Fulfillment
Poland Sp. z o.o., Wrocław

49714343R00061